Colourful Prayer

A new way to pray when words are inadequate

Sheila Julian Merryweather

kevin mayhew

Dedicated with love and thanksgiving to our
Solomon Island Sisters who helped to inspire the book

Acknowledgements

I thank all those who have continued to encourage me by their affirmation and interest, and through our workshops. I thank my Sisters in the Community of the Sisters of the Church for their support over the years and, in particular, for the generosity of Sister Susan Hird in giving her time and computer skills to the work. Thanks also to Deborah Padfield, who has helped me cross the gap between my handwritten notes and the printed word. I am grateful, too, to Joyce Huggett for all her help during the final stages of the production of this book.

The publishers wish to express their gratitude to the following for permission to include copyright material in this book:

Gollancz/Orion Publishing, for *Dibbs: In Search of Self* by Virginia Axline © 1964 Virginia Axline.

McGraw-Hill, New York, 1975, for *My Shalom, My Peace: Paintings and Poems by Jewish and Arab Children.*

First published in 2003 by
KEVIN MAYHEW LTD
Buxhall, Stowmarket, Suffolk, IP14 3BW
Email: info@kevinmayhewltd.com

KINGSGATE PUBLISHING INC
1000 Pannell Street, Suite G, Columbia, MO 65201
Email: sales @kingsgatepublishing.com

© 2003 Sister Sheila Julian Merryweather CSC

The right of Sister Sheila Julian Merryweather CSC to be identified
as the author of this work has been asserted by her in accordance
with the Copyright, Designs and Patents Act 1988.

Bible quotations are taken from the New International Version,
© Copyright 1973, 1978, 1984 by International Bible Society,
published by Hodder & Stoughton Ltd.

9 8 7 6 5 4 3 2 1
ISBN 1 84417 049 7
Catalogue No. 1500575

Design by Angela Selfe
Edited by Nick Fawcett
Printed in Great Britain

Foreword

'Tomorrow, I'd like you to *draw* in your journal rather than use words.' That challenge was given to me twelve years ago when I was on a prayer retreat. My response was to gasp and to protest in horror: 'But I can't draw!' Undaunted, my retreat-giver simply smiled and suggested that, when I felt ready, I should give it a try.

Three-quarters of the way through the retreat, I found myself stumped for words. There *were* no words to express my thoughts and feelings as I meditated on the death of Jesus *for me*. Recalling my retreat-giver's challenge, cautiously, and with little optimism, I reached for the felt-tip pens and drew a jagged shape in the middle of a page in my prayer journal. Then, choosing a different colour for each emotion that welled up inside me as I contemplated the figure of Christ on the cross, I filled the area inside the jagged frame with a variety of colours. The picture that stared up at me from my journal amazed me because it seemed to sum up so graphically the medley of emotions that clamoured for my attention at that moment. I found myself deeply moved by the experience.

When I returned home, I resorted to using words again, using colour only occasionally. Increasingly, though, over the years, colour crept back into my prayer vocabulary. I had never spoken to anyone about this so imagine my amazement when, last year, a friend wrote to me concerning a manuscript a friend of hers had written and wanted to send me on the subject of praying with colour.

The manuscript duly arrived. Before I read a single word, I thumbed through several pages and was immediately hooked. Here was someone who had given far more thought to the subject than I had ever done. Eagerly, I turned to the front page and agreed immediately with the author's claim that, when we pray, 'often colour is more helpful than words'. Fascinated, I gazed at Sheila Julian's 'colour-prayers': her orange rejoicings, her purple problems, her pleasure patterns and her expressions of anger, anxiety and peace. Such was the impact that I took seriously her suggestions and experimented for myself. The result was that, as my colour vocabulary expanded, I seemed to be set free to express myself with increasing accuracy using the medium of colour.

Like Sheila Julian, I sometimes use this method of prayer with groups. Because we live in a visual age and because colour therapy has been in vogue for a variety of reasons, few people seem to think that praying with colour is strange. Many are released by it: set free from the struggle of finding words for emotions that run so deep that no words can sum them up. So I was delighted when Kevin Mayhew agreed to publish *Colourful Prayer*. It is an invaluable and delightful primer for which many would-be pray-ers will thank God.

JOYCE HUGGETT

Introduction

I had a problem! During the years between 1983 and 1986, I found myself responsible for the training of young women of the Solomon Islands who wished to become part of the Community of the Sisters of the Church, an Anglican community. There were seventeen of them, from very different educational backgrounds. Only one had been to college. Five had had no schooling at all. The remaining eleven varied in experience from one or two years in primary school to a few years in secondary school.

This meant that their comprehension of English varied enormously. Since pidgin English had not yet become the main language of the islands, we could not even resort to this. Each island in the Solomons has its own language, and as the women came from eight different islands, some of them were unable to communicate even with each other. So I invented a ninth language!

How was I supposed to help these keen young Christian women to grow in their understanding of God and of community living, if we were unable to communicate with each other?

We did share so much. This book is the story of one tool which helped us meet with each other across the barriers of language and culture: colour. Colour became for us a means of reaching out to each other and to God. That was not the beginning of my exploration of the idea, for I had used colour for myself earlier, but it was the beginning of a bigger exploration. This book is a result of my own ongoing struggle with the understanding of prayer and its expression in relationships and life. It is my story, but it is also a story in which we all share.

Often, colour is more helpful than words. I have used it for myself and with individuals as well as groups. It is because of their response that I have felt I should try to make the experience accessible to more people. The book is made up from my notes for various workshops I have led in recent years on Colour and Spirituality.

How to use this book

If, when reading the book, you find yourself drawn to follow the suggestions interspersed throughout and discover that colour is meaningful for you, you will have found a valuable prayer tool for yourself and be in a good position to encourage others in such prayer. In addition, you will almost certainly have created your own colour code and will be able to help others to do the same in turn.

You may also find yourself in a position to lead a day's workshop on the subject. If so, you might like to consult the outline of such an event that appears in the Appendix to this book. Such workshops can inspire and release us but it is my personal belief that those finding colour helpful in this way will be guided by their own experience and exploration, and gradually grow in confidence as they exercise this God-given gift.

When you have discovered the value of colour, words will cease to be of prime importance. The colours come in the silence and speak more clearly than words. That, at least, is my own experience as well as that of many others.

I do wish you well, and hope you may be as surprised as I have been by listening to, as well as looking at and producing, colourful prayer.

Chapter 1

I believe that colour is of very real importance to each of us, but that each colour's significance is very different for each person. A colour can be diametrically opposite in its meaning for two people – hence the difficulty of choosing colours when it comes to decorating a sitting-room or bedroom!

I am convinced that how we feel about colour has a lot to do with our childhood associations. For many of us the colour yellow is a cheerful, happy one. It conjures up, perhaps, memories of seaside holidays with warm sunshine and sandy beaches. For others, however, this is not so. The colour yellow can have very grim associations. To illustrate this, I'd like to quote a passage from Virginia Axline's excellent book *Dibbs: In Search of Self* (Gollancz/Orion Publishing, 1964). In this passage, the 6-year-old boy, Dibbs, has come to the playroom and chosen to sing with the paints.

He walked over to the easel and looked at the paints. He picked up the jar of blue paint. He started to sing, and as he sang, he held up the jar of paint and moved it rhythmically, from side to side.

'Oh, paint! Oh, paint so blue!
What, oh what, is it you can do?
You can paint a sky.
You can paint a river.
You can paint a flower.
You can paint a bird.
All things are blue
if you make them blue.
Oh, blue paint, oh, paint, so blue!' . . .

He replaced this jar and picked up the red paint . . . This time he spoke the words emphatically.

'Oh, red, angry paint.
Oh, paint that scowls.
Oh, blood so red.
Oh, hate. Oh, mad. Oh, fear.
Oh, noisy fights and smeary red.
Oh, hate. Oh, blood. Oh, tears.'

He lowered the jar of red paint in his hands. He stood there silently, looking at it. Then he sighed deeply, replaced it on the easel. He picked up the yellow paint. 'Oh mean-coloured yellow,' he said. 'Oh angry, mean colour. Oh bars on windows to keep out the tree. Oh door with the lock and the turned key. I hate you, yellow. Mean old colour. Colour of prisons. Colour of being lonely and afraid. Oh mean-coloured yellow.' He put it back on the easel.

Dibbs was comfortable with the blue and green paints. The black disturbed him. He felt strongly when faced with the red. The yellow brought sadness for him in its reminders of loneliness and fear.

Another young boy from our war-torn world wrote more recently:

'I had a paint-box –
each colour glowing with delight,
I had no red for wounds or blood,
I had no black for an orphaned child,
I had no white for the face of the dead,
I had no yellow for burning sands,
I had orange for joy and life,
I had green for buds and blooms,
I had blue for clear blue skies,
I had pink for dreams and rest,
so I sat down
and painted
Peace.'

'The Paint-box' by a boy aged 9 who has known only war since he was born.
My Shalom, My Peace: Paintings and Poems by Jewish and Arab Children (McGraw-Hill, New York, 1975).

Like Dibbs, this child was unhappy with yellow. He also had very strong reasons for omitting several other colours from his paint-box, but he found peace in pink.

Each one of us, I believe, has associations attached to colours. Many of these have long been forgotten, but the relationship with the colour, once established, remains. Because of this, I have found that I am able to express myself more easily in colour than in words when something really concerns me. There are times when words fail me, but colours come to the rescue. That has been particularly true in prayer.

At one time I was in the habit of using colours for 'arrow prayers'. In the desk drawer in the office I always kept some scrap paper and felt-tipped pens. I have kept two of my favourite prayers, as they can still conjure up the feelings I had when I 'prayed' them. The first I'll call 'Thanksgiving', and the second 'Reconciliation'.

Orange seems to be the colour I reserve for very special joyful occasions. This particular morning I had received some really good news. I was so pleased that when I sat down at my desk, I was saying 'thank you, God, thank you, God' over and over again.

Thanksgiving

But somehow the words didn't seem to match what I was feeling. I wasn't aware of fishing out my colours, but there I was, producing these orange rejoicings. This colour-prayer expresses what I was really wanting to say.

We say things like 'thank you' and, in worship, 'alleluia', but I find that the words don't express all that I mean. It may be because of their frequency of use. Each colour-prayer, though, is individual. This particular 'Thanksgiving' could only be prayed once.

When I sit with it now, though, it can help me to pray other prayers of thanksgiving.

The prayer, 'Reconciliation', was again done on a scrap of paper at my desk, after having at last got back on friendly terms with a former friend.

I had been very uncomfortable for a long time, not knowing why this friend's attitude had changed towards me. That morning, we discovered it had been the result of a simple misunderstanding. We were both so relieved and glad that our relationship was restored. We could trust again.

I still feel pleasure when I revisit this prayer, and give thanks for all the relationships that flourish.

Reconciliation

Confrontation

However, I still feel uncomfortable when I come across the colour-prayer 'Confrontation' in my collection. Purple is my anxiety colour. On the morning I prayed this, I knew I had to go and confront someone. I sat at my desk praying that I'd be able to do so, it being the last thing on earth I would choose to do.

It took me a long time to get up from my chair and go to find the person concerned.

Sometimes I feel moved to use purple, but don't know why. The prayer on the right came when I was trying to understand my relationship with the colour – trying to make friends with it!

Anyone seeing these colour-prayers might think I was just doodling.

In fact, on each occasion I was praying in a way that was more real than any set prayers would have been for me. God knew what was in my heart, and in the colour we could meet.

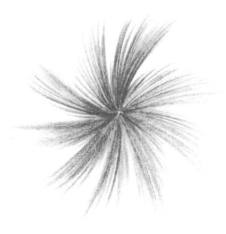

Searching

Depression

That was even more true for 'Depression', which I did when I was at a very low ebb. I could not possibly have put into words what I was feeling, but the colour did it for me.

A suggestion

Next time you have some time for quiet, pick up a colour and 'doodle' as you focus or centre on God. You may find your 'doodling' turns into praying! I suggest 'doodling' because praying with colour is not an attempt to consciously create works of art or pictures. Rather, it is a method of growing in our relationship with God that bypasses the use of words.

Chapter 2

Over the last ten years or so, I have been sharing my use of colour in prayer with many people – both with individuals and in groups varying in number from four to thirty. In our work and discussions together, we have found how very differently people feel about a colour. Sometimes we know why we associate certain colours with certain emotions, but not always.

To give you an idea of how people's experiences of colours differ, I'll list a few examples.

Green

- 'I've always loved green. We had a lovely garden with an orchard when I was small. We children spent all our holidays playing in it. They were happy times. One particular green still reminds me of the tree house we made!'
- 'I'm always comfortable with green. It was the colour of my school uniform and I was happy at school. I think that's why.'
- 'It's the opposite for me. I hated school and so I've disliked green ever since, because green was our school uniform too.'
- 'I was one of those children who wouldn't eat green vegetables. I didn't like green soup or green jelly either! I still don't like green much.'

Purple

- 'Purple always makes me sad. I think it goes back to my early nursing days. When any of the patients died, I had to put a purple cover over them.'
- 'I've always loved purple. Maybe because my Gran always wore it.'

Brown

- 'I've always felt miserable with brown. When I was small, our house had the inside walls painted brown halfway up, so that I and my brothers wouldn't spoil them. The light-coloured paper was high up.'
- 'It's my favourite colour. I grew up on a farm and loved the colour of the rich soil.'

Black

- 'I love black. It reminds me of my labrador that I had when I was small. He was my best friend.'
- 'Black is a safe colour for me. It was at night that I could escape the bullying I'd had to put up with in the daytime.'
- 'I was scared of the night – of the black. I never knew when I was going to be hurt.'
- 'I hate black. I still remember the blackout material we had during the war. The blackout meant air raids and bombs to me.'

The above are a few samples of the experiences people have had in earlier years which led to colour preferences. I have not used white in the course of this book, but for some people white is a very deliberate colour with its own unique associations.

We do not always remember why certain colours hold particular feelings for us, but we usually know which colours we need to use in given situations.

A suggestion

I'd like to suggest now that you, the reader, note down the very first colour that comes into your mind when you consider the situations outlined below. Don't stop to reason why. If you wish, you might like to use the colour on a piece of paper to express your reactions. You only need a set of felt-tips or crayons. As you've already seen from the colour-prayers, it is not a matter of producing pictures – just colour on paper. You only need a few moments for each one. See what happens. You may be surprised!

- Remember a situation that made you very angry. Can you show the anger in colour?
- Remember a time when you were very pleased. Someone, perhaps, had given you a lovely surprise or some good news. Colour?
- You might find this a harder one. You are anxious about someone or something. Colour?
- Now remember a time when you felt really peaceful. Put yourself back in that situation and see what colour comes.

In April 1998, a group of people shared in a Spirituality and Colour workshop. They kindly gave me permission to use some of their work in this book if it ever came to be written. They wanted to remain anonymous, but I'd like to say here how grateful I am to them for their generosity.

I'm going to share with you some of their responses to these same situations. As in every group I've worked with many colours were selected for each emotion.

Expressions of anger

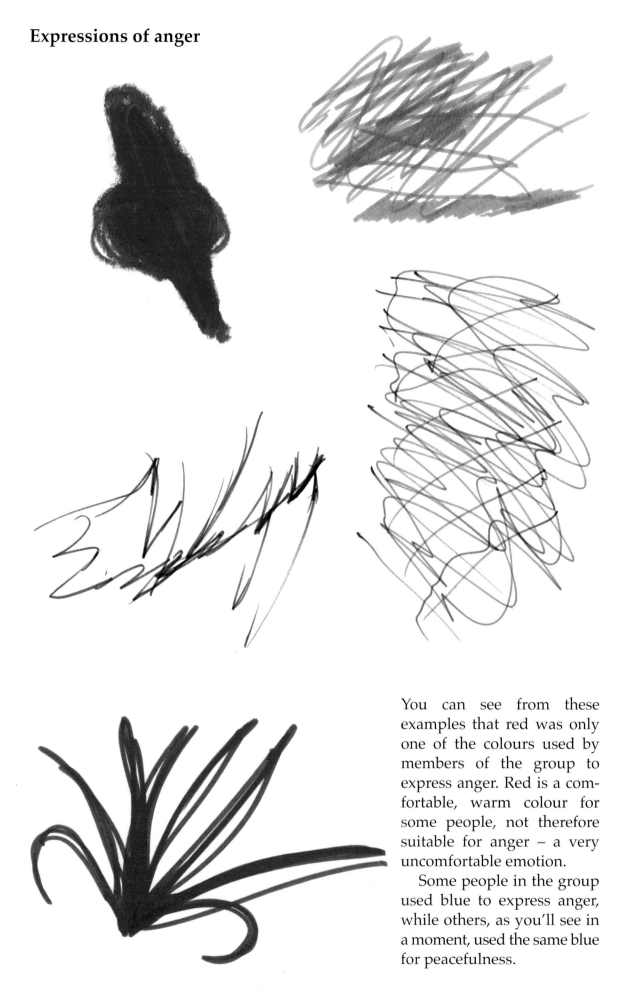

You can see from these examples that red was only one of the colours used by members of the group to express anger. Red is a comfortable, warm colour for some people, not therefore suitable for anger – a very uncomfortable emotion.

Some people in the group used blue to express anger, while others, as you'll see in a moment, used the same blue for peacefulness.

Expressions of happiness – pleasure

The green used here for happiness, and on page 15 for peacefulness, is the same as that which others had used for anger, while the yellow, which does not appear for anger, was used for all the other emotions suggested for this exercise.

It was a strange sensation for me to see purple used for happiness. Even after several years of using colour, I was still making assumptions based on my own colour work!

Expressions of anxiety

Expressions of peacefulness

Further suggestions

1. Can you colour how you are feeling now? Try to focus fully on God, using whatever way helps you: a well-known prayer . . . focusing on a candle or crucifix . . . looking at the view from your window . . . humming a well-known hymn to yourself . . . and so on. Can you add any more colours now?

2. Can you recall any early experiences which have made certain colours significant for you? Before you go on to the next chapter, see how many specific colours you can link to emotions that you experience.

Chapter 3

Because we all use colours in such varying ways, it's as though we each have an inbuilt colour code: no one can interpret our work unless we give them the key. It was this realisation that made it possible for the Solomon Island Sisters and I to communicate at long last. We needed to be able to talk to one another about our relationships within community and with our God.

In looking through the Gospels together, we realised that Jesus shares in all our emotions. Whatever our nationality, we all know anger, joy, thankfulness and so forth. God understands us and helps us to understand each other, if we are willing.

In the Solomons, we therefore agreed to use the same code as a group, while reminding ourselves that our individual codes would be different. This was the group code:

■	Depressed	▦	Lonely/sad	▦	Hopeful
▦	Afraid	▦	Disappointed	■	Trusting
▦	Anxious	▢	Peaceful	▢	Loving
▦	Angry	▦	Thankful	▨	Joyful

Obviously, we found it difficult to agree on the colours to be used, but the code did make it possible to share our feelings. We might have thought we could interpret one another's body language, but our shared, wordless journal showed us how wrong we sometimes were.

How is it possible to keep a journal without words? I'll try to explain. Let me imagine that I'm colouring my journal for yesterday. It was a busy day, as I had urgent letters to write in the morning, was meeting an old friend in the afternoon, and had to give a talk in the evening. It was not smooth sailing. There were unnecessary interruptions in the morning, a telephone call with sad news in the middle of the day, and a very long wait for the bus in the afternoon, which made me late for my friend and then late home.

I usually find that the best time to colour is first thing in the morning, as the previous day's experience has settled by then. I begin to remember/pray . . . then number the colours as they come. So, my colours for the day in question would then be

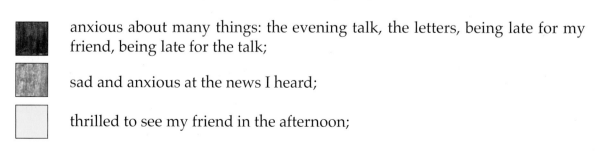

anxious about many things: the evening talk, the letters, being late for my friend, being late for the talk;

sad and anxious at the news I heard;

thrilled to see my friend in the afternoon;

 cross at the morning interruptions and the late bus;

thankful that the talk went well in the evening;

disappointed that the letters weren't finished.

Because the Solomons Sisters wanted to understand each other, we filled in a 'diary' for ten days. This, we found, was a good period as anyone who was going through a bad patch usually had a little let-up in that time.

We did it anonymously, using letters instead of names, but found in discussion that we were willing to admit to our own row.

	Sun	Mon	Tues	Wed	Thur	Fri	Sat	Sun	Mon	Tues
A										
B										
C										
D										
E										

It took a lot of trust, but was immensely worthwhile. I can see great potential for the use of such a 'diary' in marital counselling and in any relationships that are wanting to grow.

I could see from the completed 'diaries' that several of the young women were really lonely. I had imagined that I was the only one who felt that way! Those who were feeling down could see that they weren't alone, but also that the bad times didn't go on for ever. The chart enabled us to share our worries, angers and joys. We just had not realised that we all shared the same feelings. We had known it in our heads, but now we could see and believe it in our hearts.

As I said at the beginning of this chapter, we each have our own code. You will feel many things other than those listed so far: tired, excited, frustrated, eager, empty, hurt, nervous, inspired. Everything you experience belongs to your code, a particular colour representing one or many of these, just as several colours mean more than one thing to me.

A suggestion

Take time to think over, pray over, yesterday. Discover how you felt about it.

As soon as you focus on something, put down the colour that you feel is right. The very first colour that comes into your mind when you remember a situation will be the right one for you.

See if you can complete a 'day square', as I did on page 17. To encourage you, here are a few examples of other people's 'yesterday'.

 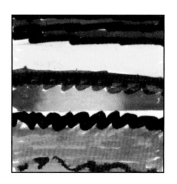 

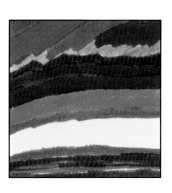 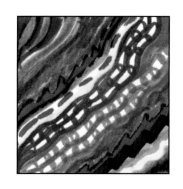 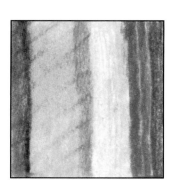

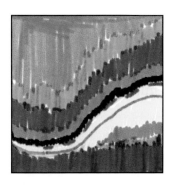  

By now, you will probably have found seven or eight of your own 'prayer-symbol-colours'. The others that you'll need can be decided in a more deliberate way. As you work with them, you'll know if you need to change them.

Your code is your own, and no one else can interpret your work. We can see in the 'yesterday' squares above that most people experienced a wide range of feelings, but we can't explain them. We don't know if the person who prayed the green, yellow and brown square had a very good day or a difficult one. All the squares keep their secrets.

Chapter 4

Some people may still be wondering how to use this colouring in prayer. I found that I had a particular 'God colour', so when I work with colour I look to see if it is there. If, after several days, I cannot see it, I deliberately use that colour on the back of my prayer. It cannot be seen – but I know it's there. Of course, God is in all colours, all life, but we need reassurance occasionally, especially when our colours worry us.

When I prayed the prayer on the left, I was bothered that God didn't seem to be in it.

So on the back I drew:

I have talked of keeping a journal in colour, and you may be wondering of what value that can be. As was shown in the colour-prayers, it is particularly helpful when we are struggling to put our feelings into words because they are too deep, too personal or simply beyond our understanding.

Here is a section of a journal I kept a few years ago.

OCTOBER					
✪ Su	1	8	15	22	29
M	2	9	16	Labour Day (NZ) 23	Marlborough Anniversary 30
T	3	10	17	24	31
W	4	11	18	25	
T	5	12	19	26	
F	6	13 Hawke's B Anniversa	20	27	
S	7	14	21	28	

I was surprised to see how much anxiety there was. However, even though it was an anxious time (purple) and at times very difficult (black, brown, grey), the journal helped to keep things in perspective, for many good things happened too (yellow, light blue, orange). I could so easily have forgotten the latter if it had been a 'wordy' journal. This way, there's no risk of forgetting.

When Christians find they spend a long time with their difficult emotions – for example, depression or fear – they can worsen the situation by adding guilt on top. It's good, therefore, to remind them – as well as ourselves – that Our Lord really does understand how it feels to be anxious or angry. He felt that way too. No one tried to tell Jesus that he was wrong to be angry or afraid, yet we are accused some-times of lacking in faith or trust, or of weakness, when we experience such feelings. We're not. We are human, as was Jesus.

To compile detailed references concerning the emotions Jesus experienced would entail another book, just as a similar exercise entailed a term's work for our Solomon Island Sisters. This chart contains their suggestions. You may find it helpful to identify other occasions when Jesus felt as you feel now.

Reminders of how Jesus shares our feelings

⬛	Depressed	'My God, my God, why have you forsaken me?' *Matthew 27:46*
⬛	Afraid	'Take this cup from me.' *Matthew 14:36*
⬛	Anxious	He wept over Jerusalem. *Luke 19:41*
⬛	Angry	With the Pharisees. In the Temple. *Matthew 23; Mark 11:15-17*
⬛	Lonely / sad	'Could you not keep watch for one hour?' *Mark 14:37*
⬛	Disappointed	Rich young man. Nine lepers. 'Don't you know me?' *Matthew 19:16-23; Luke 17:12-18; John 14:9*
⬛	Peaceful	Asleep in boat in storm. *Mark 4:35-38*
⬛	Thankful	Roman centurion. Widow's offering. *Matthew 8:5-10; Mark 12:41-44*
⬛	Hopeful	Zacchaeus. 'I will make you fishers of men.' *Luke 19:1-10; Matthew 4:19*
⬛	Trusting	'Into your hands I commit my spirit.' *Luke 23:46*
⬛	Loving	'Come to me . . .' *Matthew 11:28, 19:13-15*
⬛	Joyful	'This is my Son, whom I love; with him I am well pleased.' *Matthew 17:5*

I learned a great deal through the colour-prayer on the right. When I started it, I was in the grip of all my difficult colours – black, brown, purple and red. They are dense, and form the base. For a while, no other colours were allowed in.

As the days went by, I began to see I had let things get out of perspective. I really did have a lot to be thankful for and reasons for hope. I could begin to let go of some old resentments and to be more peaceful. Thus, gradually the other colours were allowed in.

Now, when I'm reminded of this prayer, I realise afresh how balanced life really is for me. It also reminds me of how essential the black is. Without it, this colour-prayer, and most others, would be insipid. I've needed the 'black', however unwelcome, that has come my way. It makes my life stand up.

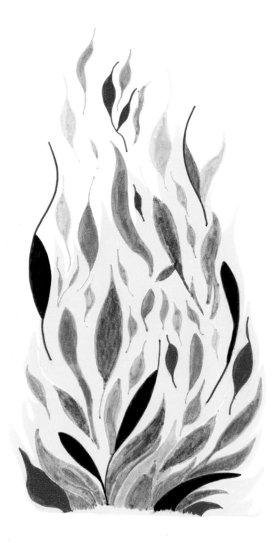

At times, one's life can seem disjointed, and yet cluttered. It can feel as if it has lost its focus.

The prayer on the left was made while I was trying to put life together again. Originally there was no yellow. Everything seemed to be all over the place. Once the yellow was admitted it made for a sense of unity; life became easier to contemplate. Yellow was the 'God-colour' which I realised must be there, in amongst it all.

Using colour in prayer can help a great deal when we are struggling with a difficult situation. It can help us to see the situation much more clearly. For example, at one time in my career, I had to move into a house and live with three other people. I found this incredibly difficult as the other three had been together for several years. I felt like an interloper. In looking through my ordinary – that is, my written – journal, I discovered that even then I'd used colour in praying about how I fitted in or could fit in.

As the prayer on the right shows, I obviously thought at the time that the other three enjoyed a close bond – everything in the garden was lovely for them, while I just felt miserable and alone.

I turned a few pages in the journal and spotted the following.

Things had improved a bit, but I was still praying about our situation. I still didn't feel I belonged, but I saw the relationships among the trio in a much more realistic way. I thought each one, at times, felt just as I did. Life wasn't all doom and gloom for me by then.

I was pleased to discover that after several more weeks had passed by, I was able to colour this.

The next colour-prayer came while spending a week in retreat, trying to face the fact that I was to be responsible for the training of four young women about whom I knew very little. I knew only that they were very different from each other.

The more I pray with colour, the more I realise how unique is each individual person. As I prayed about each member of this group, I coloured as I saw them and myself. I could not imagine how we were to form a relating group. The longer I prayed, though, the more the connections were gradually made. It ceased to be five sections, and became one whole. The primary colours were there for each of us – even the yellow is there, hidden in the green and brown. Blue and red are more easily seen, and black is present throughout.

This prayer didn't take away the apprehension I felt, but it did help.

The three colour-prayers or meditations below belong together. They took place when I was struggling through a bad patch. I think you'll be able to see how prayer in colour helped to alleviate the situation.

15 May: I was in the grip of fear, anger and a felt nothingness.

17 May: I was still experiencing the anger, fear and nothingness but not as intensely. Light was coming in.

19 May: Now the nothingness, anger and fear were still there at the centre, but not in control. They were contained and balanced by other elements.

A suggestion

If something is worrying you, next time you pray about it have your piece of paper and colours nearby. Try using them as you pray.

Chapter 5

I needed a way of using colour in the day-to-day quiet time. I therefore started to keep within easy reach the set of colours that I use, and ready drawn circles of various sizes. In this way, if I felt drawn to colour as I prayed, there was no disruption. I could just reach out for the paper and colours.

Months go by when I do not use colour, but when something is bothering me then the felt-tips come to the rescue. I may find I need to use them for several consecutive days while working through a situation. At other times, a once-off may do the trick.

This way of praying may be difficult for artists as they can be too deliberate in their work. For me, it's more like a dream experience. The colours take over in the prayer and it can often take several days before what I have produced speaks to me – or before God reaches out to me through the coloured circle.

When I first started using colour, I used to spread the colours out over a page, usually beginning at the base. The use of a circle was suggested to me when I went on a colour weekend. I had been scared of going, afraid that my own feelings about colour might be undermined. In the course of the weekend we were introduced to 'mandalas', which are circular, with very definite rules that have to be followed – for example, beginning in the middle. How could I transpose my colour into a circle by starting at the centre?

Then I realised that, while my circles did not need to be mandalas, putting my colours in a circle was helpful. The circle is a symbol of completeness, with no beginning and no ending. However large or small, it is still complete. I feel safe within the circles I draw. They give me boundaries.

I thus moved from this . . .

to this . . .

25

I am at the centre of my life – my circle – but for me to exist at all, God has to be at the centre of my centre. So all life flows out from God to me and through me, as well as from the centres of all the people I meet and through them. All our lives – our circles – are held together in the whole circle of God's love.

Experimenting with the circle in prayer, I have found that God really does use it to reach me; and I use it to reach God.

The circular prayer on the previous page provides another reminder of how impossible it is to interpret someone else's work. Several people who saw the circle, not having seen the 'flat' expression on the left, remarked how attractive it was. To me it was the opposite. The colours I had used were disturbing ones for me, and the end result reminded me of a mangrove swamp, the last place in which I'd want to be. I had been praying about a difficult situation from which I was trying to extricate myself. The circle was the expression of that colour-dream-prayer experience.

For some people, it's the pattern rather than the colour that speaks. I'm not attempting in this book to explain the relationship between the use of colour and the shape or pattern. I know there must be one, but it's the colour that's helpful for me. That doesn't mean, though, that pattern is irrelevant. Some colour-prayers do come out more like 'pictures'. I did the one below in a time of struggle. Afterwards, I sat down to work out what it meant.

- I always seem to be in a fog of not understanding anything about the present.
- There's so much I don't know.
- I am just going on being true to self and what I have known to be true in the past.
- I can always see in retrospect that God – the Holy Spirit – has been there, in control.

A suggestion

Most of my 'circle-prayers' take about an hour. Set an hour aside for yourself and God and deliberately decide to use colour in a circle during this time to help you in your prayer time. Just relax with God and use the colours as they come into your mind. (If the colours don't come, don't force them – it may not be the right time for you. I certainly don't always use them.)

Chapter 6

In addition to helping with personal problems or worries, praying with colour can help with the understanding of wider themes.

How many of us have wrestled with the meaning of Good Friday? Does it really deserve to be called 'Good'? With colour, I can grasp a little more than I ever can with words. The colour sets it more clearly in context than words can do.

C. The day of resurrection burst forth and all was renewed.

B. Holy Saturday followed. A time of desolation.

A. Here I can see that all suffering, all life, was held in Our Lord's offering on the cross.

These colour-prayers, or meditations, still remain more helpful to me than reading books on the subject. Of course, we need to study, but the colour helps to express our understanding of what we read.

Occasionally the Church presents us with a symbol which is not at all helpful. The very last symbol I would choose to represent the Holy Spirit is fire. Yes, of course it's a natural one to be chosen in view of the account in Acts 2, but I'm sure I'm not the only one who has had very unpleasant experiences of fire. All the symbol does is rekindle these memories. How many of us as children saw devastation wrought by incendiary bombs? How many people have had to fight fires as I have done in Borneo and the Solomons in their dry seasons? We have seen on our television screens recently the horrifying bushfires in Australia around Sydney and Canberra. Far too often we hear of homes destroyed and lives lost as a result of fire.

When we are not helped by a certain symbol, it is good to create our own. I put up my own symbol to counteract the red flame of fire during the season of Pentecost, seeing the Holy Spirit instead as wind, water and life.

A suggestion

Why not try your hand at meditating in colour on the themes of Christmas or Ascensiontide? See what comes . . .

Chapter 7

Finally, I want to include a few more examples of colour-prayer-meditations – call them what you will – which came to me while writing.

You'll see from all the prayers in this book that there's no wrong or right way of using colour. I have found a way that has been helpful to me and to some others. You will find your own way, if colour holds meaning for you.

In this one on the left, yellow is the colour of love, red represents anger, black hatred and purple is either suffering or healing – I wasn't sure which.

I prayed it at a time when I was trying to believe that God's love was strong enough to hold the world, and us, together. Would we grow towards wholeness or disintegration?

Often, it is when I revisit prayers that God can speak to me through them. This is probably because, when I produce them, I'm colouring 'my side of the story'. I need to step back later for God to come through to me.

Do we ever stop asking questions? I don't think so. I was feeling swamped by doubts when I offered the prayer on the right, but as the prayer continued and I meditated on the words 'I do believe; help me overcome my unbelief!' (Mark 9:24), so I was able to see that the questions came out from a tapestry of life that did contain some certainty – at least enough to hold the questions.

Like the previous one, if this prayer had been tackled in words, I would still be writing!

While the next prayer was in progress, I was trying to sort out relationships.

Many of the colours, although looking alive and peaceful, never seem to meet up with each other. The purple is the colour that unites, but although I know when I need to use it, I'm still not sure what I'm conveying when I do so.

Occasionally, as with all prayer, I'm left waiting, not knowing. I was bothered when the prayer below came to be. It's full of my disturbing colours. However, there's some hope at the centre, with the green.

I had no idea of how to complete this circle, and it's right that I left it. It would not have been a genuine prayer if I had just filled the space with a 'comfortable' colour.

It seems appropriate to end with this unfinished prayer. In God's good time, the space may be filled – or I may never know the answer. Maybe that's how it should be.

Postscript

Occasionally a person will find that their colour-prayer brings more to the surface than anticipated. We never know when God will bring disturbing memories or insights into our consciousness. I am sure this only happens when we are ready to deal with them, but if this happens it may be necessary to seek professional help from a trained counsellor or therapist.

Appendix

An Outline Plan for a Day's Workshop

Morning

A. Introduction

1. Share with the group your own experience of working with colour in prayer (see pages 7-9).
2. Check that each member of the group has his or her own set of colours.
3. Give each person four or five pieces of A5 paper so that they are prepared to colour the kind of situations mentioned on page 11.
4. Give participants time to complete this exercise in silence. Tell them how many minutes they will have to complete each part of the exercise.
5. When the exercise has been completed, encourage group members to share what they have created with the group. This way, everyone can see for themselves the variety of colours selected for any given feeling.
6. Put up a colour code for all to see but stress that each individual will have different emotions in their list and each person will also choose different colours to represent different emotions (see page 16 and the final paragraph of page 17).
7. Remove the code and encourage the group to draw up their own colour code.

B. Praying with Colour

1. Help the group to pray over their 'yesterday' (see Chapter 3).
2. If possible, share your own 'yesterday' with the group before asking group members to do so.
3. Note that squares of 30-40 cm should be big enough for this exercise.
4. Stress that no one's square can be interpreted unless it is shared by the person concerned.
5. Note that, although group-sharing can be very helpful, unless members of the group know each other, such sharing might best be left until later in the day.

Coffee Break

C. Development

1. Mention the value of keeping a daily record in colour (see page 20).

2. Invite members of the group to suggest ways in which Jesus obviously experienced the kinds of feelings that are part of our make-up (see page 21). Some groups will be ready to enter into this exercise with enthusiasm. Others may not be ready for this approach.

3. Show how colour can help us when we are living through tricky situations – like the one mentioned on pages 22-23. Use illustrations of your own if you possibly can; they may be more pertinent to your particular group.

4. For the remainder of the morning, suggest that group members find a quiet place where, armed with paper and colours, they can relax with God. Suggest that, having relaxed in his presence, they hand over their worries to him and, as they pray, translate some of their prayer into colour. Emphasise that the colours should not be forced but should rather just be allowed to flow if they will. Explain that, when using colour, we don't make a conscious decision to use this or that colour or to draw this or that shape – what we put on paper becomes more like a 'dream' experience.

5. By this stage of the day, some members of the group might appreciate a larger piece of paper so make sure you have some available.

Afternoon

1. Now that the group has had the opportunity to experiment, explain that containing our colour within a circle can be helpful because it 'holds' our prayer (see page 25 and top of page 26).

2. If possible, share your own circles with the group. There are examples on pages 24, 25, 29 and 30 if you need them.

3. Give the group between 45 minutes and one hour to create their own circles and/or to continue the work they began during the morning session.

Conclusion

By this time, the group should have gelled, so encourage individuals to share how it felt to work with colour and to show members of the group what they have created. Each person will gain a great deal from this kind of sharing.

Further Suggestions

If there is time, other projects could be introduced as suggested in Chapter 6, for example,

*   creating symbols for Pentecost
*   creating symbols for other festivals
*   creating symbols for special family or community occasions
*   creating personal symbols.

Some groups and individuals will find that this last exercise is a more manageable 'way in' to the use of colour than using it as prayer – a thought worth bearing in mind as you prepare for the day.